# The Coastal Path Note Book

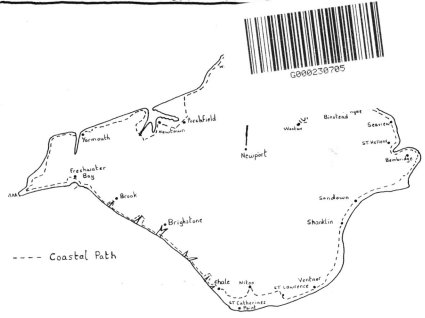

Porchfield · Newtown · Yarmouth · Freshwater Bay · Brook · Brighstone · Chale · Niton · ST Lawrence · ST Catherines Point · Ventnor · Shanklin · Sandown · Bembridge · ST Hellens · Seaview · Binstead · Ryde · Wooton · Newport

---- Coastal Path

# The Coastal Path Note Book

## Introduction

The Isle of Wight Coast Path covers a variety of walking delights in its 70 miles, from Victorian seaside towns such as Ryde and Shanklin to the rugged and often remote cliffs of the South West coast.

This note book has been written for the walk in an anticlockwise direction for four reasons:

1 By completing sections 1 & 2 the road walking is done first.

2 A semi-rural route for the first few miles allows the newcomer a chance to find his or her feet and to grasp map reading on our and o/s maps before slightly more rural instructions are given.

3 The North side of the Island is largely protected from the South West winds, so going into the wind is acceptable.
On the S.W. coast, however, it is wise to have the wind to your back and hence the S.E or anticlockwise direction.

4 Its the way we chose to walk it.

Take the route slowly, allowing time to stop and view or explore to your satisfaction the features mentioned, and those you find for yourself.

## The Coast

It should be stressed that parts of the Islands Coast are subject to erosion and that if danger or trespass are suspected the path should be left, and re-joined at the next available point having traversed a safer alternative route.

## Kit List

First and foremost are a pair of comfortable shoes or boots, secondly a waterproof jacket and trousers, and a rucksack to carry your belonging in.

From here on its up to you, but the following items may help your thoughts:

First Aid kit, change of clothes (it is a weeks walk after all!) camera, flask, lunch box

(2)

# Using the Guide

This guide is divided into six sections/days with the maps of the route on the left page and the relevant points of interest, where possible, on the facing page.

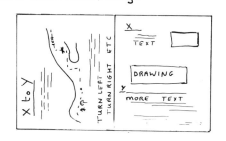

## Maps

The maps are of a continuous strip format, and are drawn to approximately 2½ inches to the mile.
The start and finish of each map is marked by a ⓢ and Ⓕ respectively, along with the instructions to walk the section.
It is advised that the Ordnance Survey Map Outdoor Leisure 29 be used in conjunction with the guide so that an overall picture of distance and relief can be obtained.

| | |
|---|---|
| – – – – Main Coast Path | ▫ Buildings |
| .–.–.– Alternative route | ꝟ Wet Land/Marsh |
| ‗‗‗ Main road | ⟶ Stream/bridge/Lake |
| ‗‗‗ Minor rd/track/made up path. | A Fingerboard |
| | ⊓⊓⊓ Cliff Face |
| ·········· Fence/hedge | Area of slumping or cliff fall |
| ⚰ Church | ↟ Trees |
| | –x–-I–- Stile, Gate (on path) |

To assist with navigation the details from the finger-boards has been recorded and is included on the map page.

It would be wise to put this note book in a map case or clear plastic bag so that it is kept clean and dry so that:
(a) It can be read if it rains
(b) You dont have to buy another one ....... on second thoughts!

# The Coastal Path, a personal note

Whilst paths exist that start or finish at the coast, the Isle of Wight Coastal Path is one of the few long distance paths that completely encircles a landmass. One advantage of which is that by returning to the start point, travel arrangements are simplified.

This note book is an account of our findings and the route that we followed on the Coastal Path.

In the course of the 70 miles travelled, a large part of the Island was explored, a proportion of which are quiet and beautiful places that the car driver will doubtless miss.

The studies of the Island can be as varied as history, geography, politics, famous people, ornithology, geology and botany to name but a few.
The exploration of these subjects, to any depth, are books in themselves so whilst some of the topics are touched upon there is plenty more reading should you wish to.

We enjoyed our days on the Island and hope you do also.

Pyramid and Bee Orchids, two of the less known Island attractions.

The Needles, one of the well known Island attractions.

(4)

# Section 1
## Ryde to East Cowes

### 8 Miles

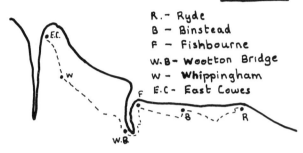

R. - Ryde
B - Binstead
F - Fishbourne
W.B - Wootton Bridge
W - Whippingham
E.C - East Cowes

If you are following the suggestion in the introduction then this is the first section of the walk from Ryde Pier and the ferry.

The route to Fishbourne takes you through residential areas and across a golf course to the Norman Church at Binstead. From Binstead the route passes the Quarr Abbeys, occupied and derelict, to Fishbourne and the thought that in a few miles nearly one thousand years of history has been seen. From the pretty village of Fishbourne the route navigates Wootton Creek and the village to emerge at Palmers Farm where the Brocks Copse Road is followed to Whippingham. Views from the road of the Solent are good especially at the Wootton end before descending to the Brocks Copse and Palmers Brook, however do keep an eye out for traffic as no path is present.

From Whippingham to East Cowes the route follows the main rd, the coast not being accessible, past Barton Manor and Osborne House.

On reaching East Cowes the path continues through the main street, York Ave, before arriving at the jetty on Ferry Road for the Chain Ferry to West Cowes and the completion of this section.

# Ryde Pier to Wootton Bridge

To start your journey, from the pier turn right toward the tourist information office go around the roundabout and turn right into St Thomas Street. As the road begins to climb Buckingham Rd to the right and then to the left to meet with Spencer Rd. Turn right and follow Spencer Rd to the junction, beside a gate, of Ryde Golf Course and the A3054. Turn half right ...... (Fb-A) along the hedge lined path crossing the golf course, over the footbridge and on to Binstead Church.

On leaving the church walk straight ahead for 100yds, before turning right into Church Rd which is then followed around to the left until a bridleway is seen on your right. (Fb-B) Turn right and proceed until a path to the left, (Fb-c) beside a house, is taken through the woods to emerge onto Quarr Road. Turn right and continue on this rd, which leads into a track, until the remains of the original Quarr Abbey can be seen around you.

Continue along the track, under the archway to the new abbey, (Fb-D) and finally the junction with Fishbourne Lane.

Turn left, past the ferry terminal, until a phone box and Fingerboard (Fb-E) are seen on your right. Turn right and take the path to Ashlake Copse Rd, and then turn left. At the next junction take the path through the woods and continue until the main rd is reached. Turn right for Wootton Bridge.

Fingerboards

(A) P.F.P. R48 Binstead and Quarr    (B) B.w to Quarr and Fishbourne    (C) P.B.W. Fishbourne.

(D) P.B.W R3 Fishbourne and beach    (E) P.F.P R1 Kite hill.

Map labels:

- take follow ...... (Fb-A)
- ST THOMAS STREET
- BUCKINGHAM ROAD
- SPENCER ROAD
- A3054
- N
- BINSTEAD CHURCH
- GOLF COURSE
- CHURCH RD
- NEW ABBEY
- OLD ABBEY AND ARCHWAY
- QUARR RD
- FISHBOURNE LANE
- ASHLAKE COPSE RD

## Ryde

On arrival at the pier head, via the catamaran, the view of Ryde is of a Victorian sea-side town set in to the hillside, the influence of which is very apparent in the style and type of the buildings, the most obvious being the near half mile long pier.

Ryde was originally two small villages, the lower, coastal being a fishing community and the upper, inland being farming joined by what is now Union St and the High St.

The pier, built in 1824, and added to as needs demanded, has provided a regular foot passenger link with the mainland and hence road and rail since 1826 by using the facility for mooring regardless of high or low tide.

### Binstead Church

A quiet picturesque church at the northern end of Binstead village, the site originating from Norman times, indeed the gate way in the boundary wall and the gargoyle dates from that period. The main construction of the church is of Victorian build with repair work added after fire damaged parts in 1969, evidence of which can be seen by the scorch marks on some of the pews.

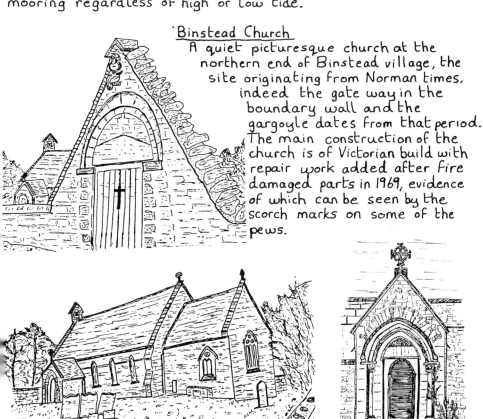

# Wootton Bridge to Whippingham

From the bridge cross the Sloop Inn P.H. forecourt to a track. Ahead of you take the path along side the Unity Hall building. On reaching a road turn right and continue, keeping an eye out for a school on your left.

Turn left into School Lane and follow the path that goes around to the right, (Fb-A) at the back of some houses.

### Fingerboard
(A) P.F.P. N97 Church Rd via ST Edmund walk.

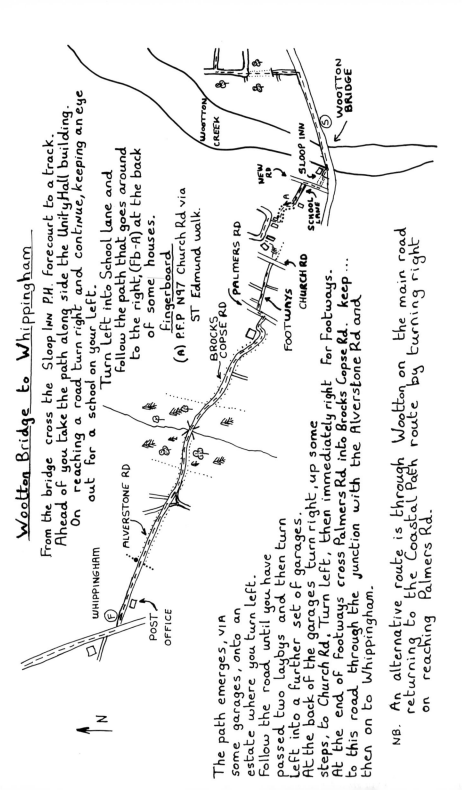

The path emerges, VIA some garages, onto an estate where you turn left. Follow the road until you have passed two laybys and then turn left into a further set of garages. At the back of the garages turn right, up some steps, to Church Rd. Turn left, then immediately right For Footways. At the end of Footways cross Palmers Rd into Brocks Copse Rd. keep... to this road through the junction with the Alverstone Rd and then on to Whippingham.

NB. An alternative route is through Wootton on the main road returning to the Coastal Path route by turning right on reaching Palmers Rd.

# The Abbeys

Quarr Abbey_ or more to the point, the remains of it, can be seen on both sides of the track.

Dating from the 12th Century, and built by Cistercian monks, the abbey owes its demise principally to King Henry VIII who in the 16th Century dissolved the monasteries.

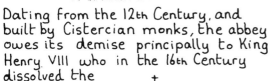

The present abbey, further along the track, was built in 1912 by Benedictine Monks, with its red brick work clearly standing out in the well kept surroundings.

## Fishbourne

Situated on the eastern side of Wooton Creek it is perhaps best known for the car ferry, but behind the busy port is a very pretty village dating back to the 14th Century.

Spare the time for a deviation to the village green and shoreline..... its well worth it.

(9)

# Whippingham to East Cowes Chain Ferry

From the road junction turn right along the A3021 toward East Cowes.
Continue along the path, passing Barton Manor and Osbourne House on your right.
The approach to the Floating bridge is via the main street, York Ave where a left turn in to Ferry Road concludes this section at the chain ferry.

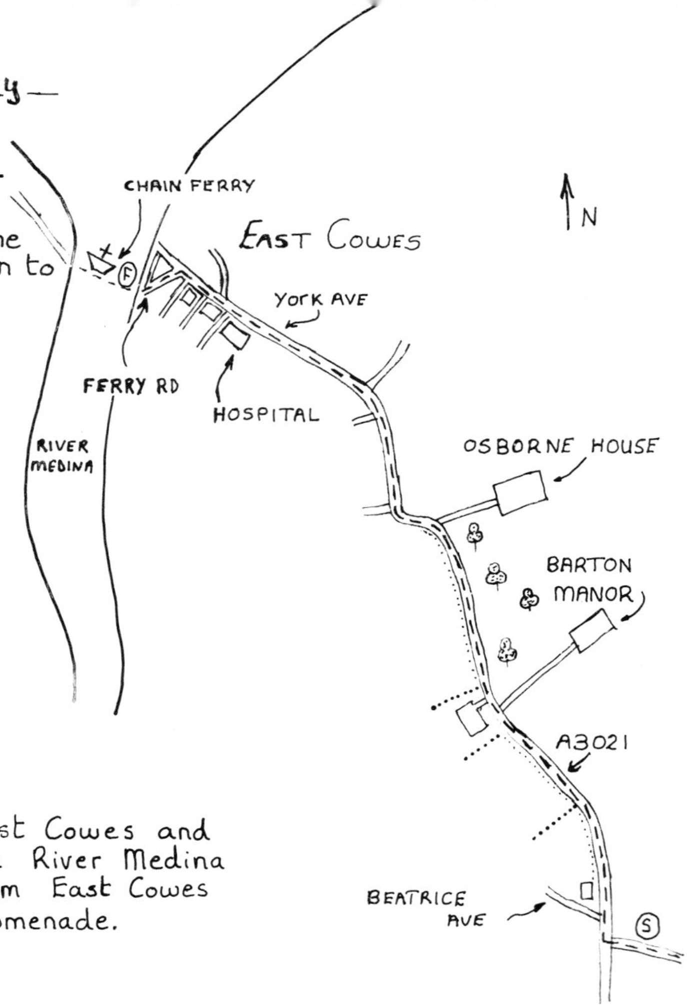

If East Cowes is your overnight stop, then a walk along the promenade is a very pleasant end to the day.

In addition to the promenade stroll, both East and West Cowes have some tasty Fish and chip shops.

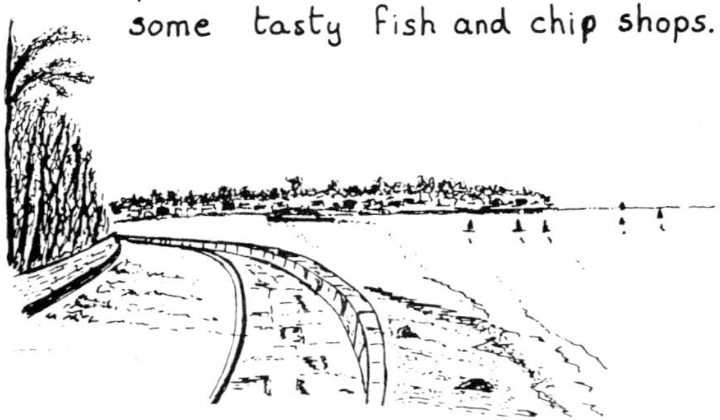

N

CHAIN FERRY

EAST COWES

YORK AVE

HOSPITAL

FERRY RD

RIVER MEDINA

OSBORNE HOUSE

BARTON MANOR

A3021

BEATRICE AVE

West Cowes and the River Medina from East Cowes promenade.

## Wootton Bridge

.... looking South at the Old Mill Pond, which is Fed by Blackbridge and Chillingwood Brooks

.... and looking North at the busy, tidal creek.

## Whippingham

The route along the Whippingham Road does allow splendid views of Newport, the River Medina and the central chalk downs. Although not on the Coastal Path, the church of ST Mildred along Beatrice Ave is an excellent detour, for its location, views, and history.

## Osborne House

was the island home of Queen Victoria, and where she subsequently died in Jan of 1901.

The chain ferry linking East and West Cowes across the River Medina.

# The Solent and River Medina.

Since the conclusion to this section is the view of the Solent and River Medina, perhaps a note about their formation is appropriate.

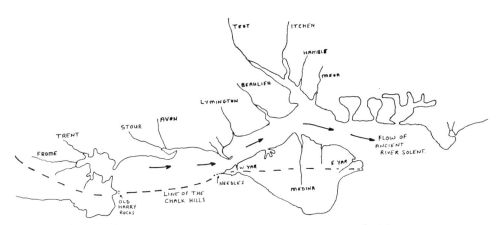

The area that we now know as the Isle of Wight was once part of Mainland Southern England and extended further to the South than the present Southern coast.
The shaping began some 1 million years ago with the coming of the last ice age.
The ice sheets that covered huge areas of the globe required water, to freeze, so the sea levels fell world wide. This drop in sea levels meant that the rivers that flowed across the land deepened their valleys to reach the coastline, an example of which is the then River Solent which flowed Eastward.
When the ice began to melt and retreat the resultant rise in sea levels caused the river valleys to slowly flood, and the River Solent became a sea. (about 8 to 10,000 years ago)
It is also this rise in sea levels that assisted the process of eroding the chalk ridge between the Island and the Mainland to finally separate the two. (about 3,500 years ago)
The formation of the Solent has produced both shallow and deep water harbours making it serviceable with commercial shipping and small boat owners alike.
The Solent is relatively sheltered, however, unusual tides, currents and winds have claimed many ships, indeed the Admiralty chart "Solent Approaches" has some 4,000 wrecks listed. The Mary Rose which sank in 1545 has now been salvaged and is being restored at Portsmouth Harbour.

(12)

# Section 2
## West Cowes to Yarmouth

w.c. — West Cowes
G — Gurnard
T — Thorness
P — Porchfield
N — Newtown
S — Shalfleet
Y — Yarmouth

18 Miles

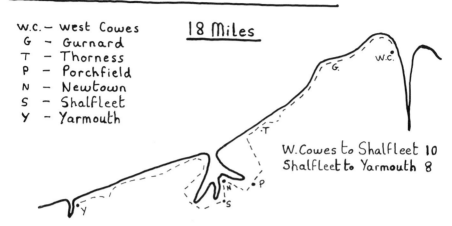

W. Cowes to Shalfleet 10
Shalfleet to Yarmouth 8

This long section may be broken into two shorter sections by an overnight stop at Porchfield or Shalfleet.

A short walk through W Cowes town precinct to the Victoria Parade, and then a further two miles of unobscured Solent views to Gurnard starts section 2 magnificently.

The first real experience of coastal erosion is from Gurnard Bay to Thorness Bay.

When you reach the beach turn around to see the effects of the cliff slumping.

Inland now, through the Holiday Camp, and S. Thorness Farm to the road and Porchfield.

More roads to Newtown and the Estuary, and on to Shalfleet.

From Shalfleet the path navigates the Estuary to the coast at Hamstead.

The coastal path continues over Bouldnor Cliff top, through Bouldnor Copse, with splendid views of coast and a variety of wildlife for the quiet and eagle eyed.

Finally the last leg of the road from Bouldnor Hamlet to the sea wall and into Yarmouth.

(13)

# West Cowes Chain Ferry to Thorness Bay

From the chain Ferry take Medina Rd until a left hand bend where Birmingham Rd is taken to the right, this leads into the pedestrian High St. At the end of two pedestrian sections is the post office and at the next junction the Union Inn P.H. and Watchhouse Lane where a right turn is made for the seafront and Victoria Parade.

Turn left and take the coastal path past the Royal Yacht Squadron and on to Egypt Point. Follow the sea wall to Gurnard Bay.

Stay on the promenade until you pass a parade of changing huts, on your left, continuing until a boat slipway. Turn left and climb the hill until the junction with Shore Rd is reached where the footpath, half right is taken.

At the end of the path turn right and follow the road around to the left. Turn right into Solent View Road, which leads into Marsh Rd and on over Gurnard Bridge where you turn right, infront of Marsh Cottage.

Turn left on to the coastal path of which the first part (Fb-A) is between fence on the left, bushes and coast on the right.

When a stile is reached, on your left, marked with a yellow arrow pointing right, cross into the field turning immediately right and follow around the edge exiting by the cliff top path and a stile.

The path now twists and turns as the descent to Thorness Bay is made.

(A) Coastal path CS16

### Fingerboard
Thorness 1  Porchfield 3

EGYPT POINT

N

ROYAL YACHT SQUADRON

WATCH HOUSE LANE

HIGH ST

MILL HILL RD

BIRMINGHAM RD

MEDINA RD

GURNARD BAY

SHORE RD

SOLENT VIEW RD

MARSH RD

MARSH COTTAGE

YELLOW WAYMARKER

THORNESS BAY

## West Cowes.

The area of W. Cowes is perhaps best known for its maritime activities, which includes ferries to the mainland, numerous moorings, a maritime museum and the home of Cowes Week.

Cowes Week is a sailing and boating regatta that attracts many people and craft to the island, and is based around the promenade and Royal Yacht Squadron Club House.

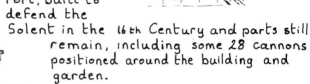

The original use of the club house building was of a fort, built to defend the Solent in the 16th Century and parts still remain, including some 28 cannons positioned around the building and garden.

## Egypt Point

For anyone who is ticking them off, this is the most Northerly point of the island and the start of the North-West coast.

Egypt Point is marked by a small lighthouse and a stone lion, erected by the local board of health in 1894, and is also the sight of a submarine boom going across the Solent to Stone Point, a Southern peninsula on the mainland, during World War Two.

## Gurnard

For the coastal path walker, Gurnard is an inland deviation from the promenade, but with superb views (once Shore Rd has been climbed!) before returning to the coast at Gurnard Luck on the Western side of the bay. (15)

Coastal Path CS16
Thorness Bay 1
Porchfield 3

# Thorness Bay to Porchfield

Cross the sands and take the track,(Fb-A), to the left up to, and through the holiday camp until the entrance is reached. Just before a car ramp look for the coastal path fingerboard (Fb-B) and turn right up a tree lined path.

When a stile and field are seen on the left, via a gap in the hedge, turn left and cross to a road.

Turn Left (Fb-C) and follow the road around to the right where a path (Fb-d) is taken across a small field.

Turn left just beyond the hedge and follow the line of the fields, and through two gates, to the Porchfield Road.

Turn right and follow the road to Porchfield.

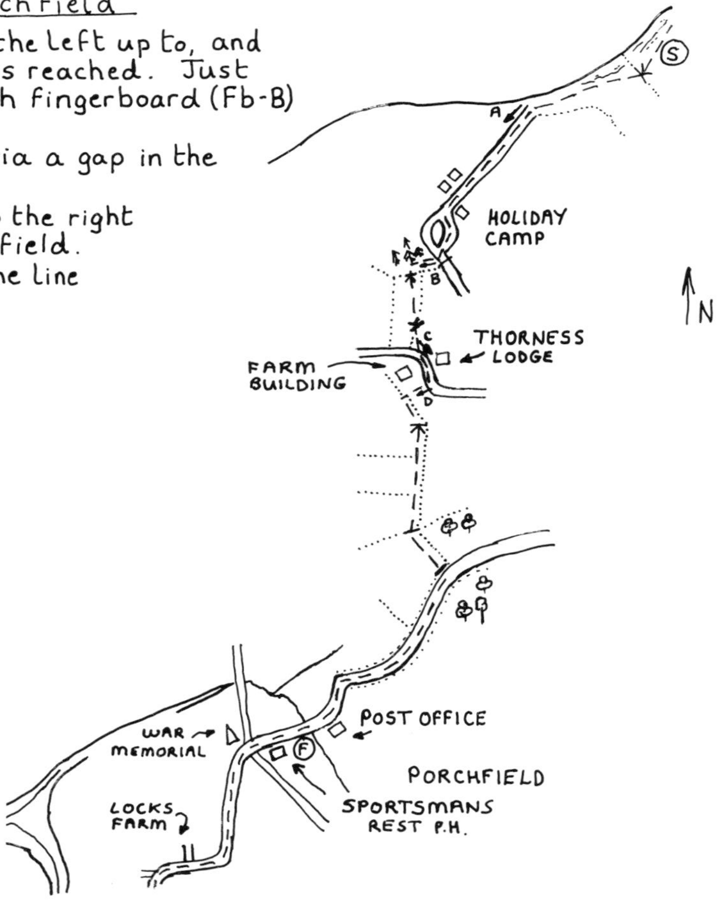

### Fingerboards

(A) (B) (C) Coastal path
(D) P.F.P. CB12a Porchfield ½

Thorness Bay from the holiday camp.

N

## Thorness Bay.

The rather collapsible path that you have just made your way down can now **be** explained .... by looking N.E and S.W. from the beach the extent of the cliff erosion, a combination of the —

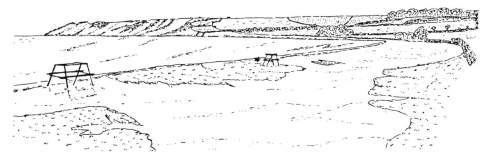

— layering of the rocks and the relentless action of the sea can be seen.

This bay is popular with ornithologists as the combination of marsh land, mud flats and sands brings many varieties of birds.

### Porchfield

A small collection of houses, a post office, pub and store mark the delightful village of Porchfield on our route.

Rodge Brook, the stream beside the store, is one of the tributaries to Clamerkin Lake which is a major feature of the next few miles.

The same is true of Clamerkin Brook to be crossed by bridge a half mile out of the village.

Porchfield can be an over night stop, and if so then another view of Rodge brook can be achieved by following the lane beside the memorial.

(17)

# Porchfield to Hamstead Farm

Continue on the rd, over Clamerkin Bridge, until the rd to Newtown is taken on the right. As the rd bends to the right, past Old Vicarage Lane, after 150 yds a path (Fb-A) is taken to the left. A series of small wooden posts marks the route across the fields, and will emerge via a hedge lined track, at Newtown. Turn left, past the Town Hall, over Newtown Bridge and on to the rd junction, turn right and walk along the rd until Corf Farm. Turn right, along the track to Shalfleet Mill. Turn right along the woodland path and follow around to the left crossing the bridge. Turn left and follow the track to Shalfleet.

At the T junction, New Inn PH on right, turn right along the rd, keep walking until you see a fingerboard on the right (Fb-b). Turn right and follow around the field, keeping to the right until you see a bridge, cross the bridge. A slight left bias on the wooded path will emerge onto a track (Fb-c)

Turn right, over Ningwood Lake Bridge, and continue until the Coastal Path track to the right (Fb-d) is taken for Newtown Estuary. On reaching the estuary look for (Fb-e) on your left, just after the wooded path. Turn left along the fenced path and follow around the waters edge to the corner of a field, way-marker on tree on the left. Follow the left side of the field to a stile, cross over, and turn half right for the opposite corner and a wood bridge.

Continue ahead to the coast. Turn left along the beach for Hamstead Point. Turn left up the track for Hamstead Fm.

## Fingerboards

(A) F.P. Newtown CB13a

(b) C.P S11 Lower Hamstead and Yarmouth 6¼

(c) C.F.P. S27 Lower Hamstead 1¼ (S28)

(D) C.F.P S28 and Hamstead trail

(E) C.F.P. S3 H/stead, Bouldnor Yarmouth 5

N

NEWTOWN

TOWN HALL

NEWTOWN BRIDGE

VICARAGE LANE

MOD

CLAMERKIN BRIDGE AND BROOK

(S)

CORF FM

SHALFLEET

NEW INN PH

NINWOOD LAKE

CREEK FM

## Newtown

The coastal path does not actually pass through Newtown, but gets so close that to miss this beautiful village would make the road walking of the last miles seem pointless.

The origins of Newtown, once the island capital, date to the 13th century but the years and a french raid, in the 14th century, have altered the town significantly.

By walking through the village the estuary can be reached at both Clamerkin and Causeway lakes giving splendid views of village and coast.

In addition the church and village water pump make for interesting reading and viewing.

The Town Hall, built in 1699 and subsequently re-built in 1933 after it fell into disrepair is now open to the public at certain times, and contains a museum.

## Causeway Lake Bridge.

The view and close proximity of the lake are excellent .... but the longer you stay, and the quieter you are... the more you will see.

## Shalfleet

A small village on the A3054, Shalfleet is a worthy pause, and if W. Cowes to Yarmouth is too much in one go then quite likely an over night stop.

In the village is a watermill, pub, Church of ST Michael the Archangel, and the tributary Caul Bourne flowing to Shalfleet lake.

## Shalfleet Church

is a fascinating step into history going back to the 11th century. The time is well spent by savouring the photographs, pictures, architecture and atmosphere.

# Hamstead Farm to Yarmouth

Continue through the farm on the track (Fb-A) until the track bends to the left, where a path is taken to the right, over a stile (Fb-B) and across 4 fields, the last one diagonally. **Keep right** infront of West Hamstead Farm, a fingerboard with no words points in the correct direction to the corner of the field. Follow the path and track to the tracks junction, turn left (Fb-C). Continue and look for a fingerboard and track, West Close on the right (Fb-D), turn right and follow until a path is seen on the left. Turn left and follow the path around a property on the right, and then keep right along the line of the field for Bouldnor Copse. Stay on the wooded cliff top path, until a small bay is reached. Leave the bay by the woodland path, right at the Y junction and then left for 300 yds to the fingerboard (Fb-E) and plank bridge.

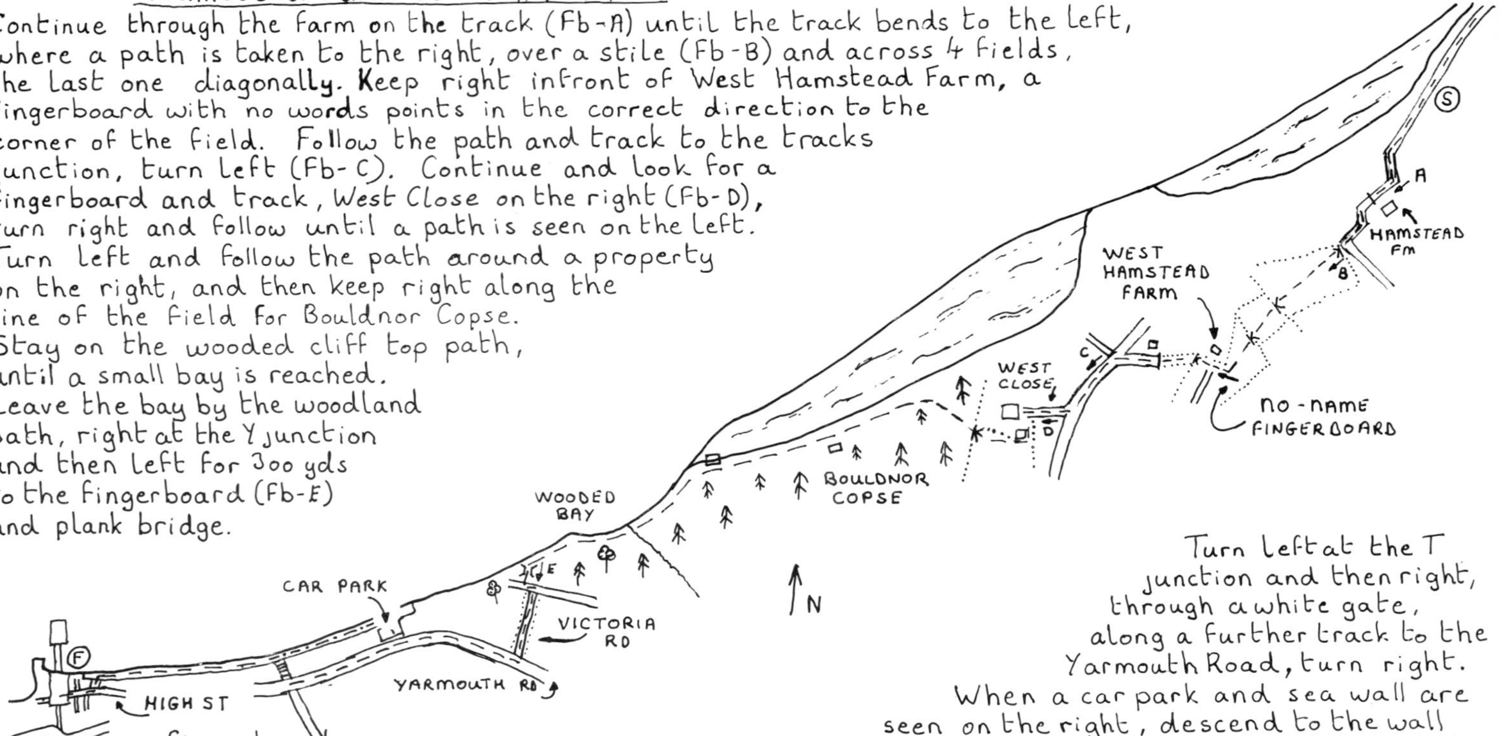

Turn left at the T junction and then right, through a white gate, along a further track to the Yarmouth Road, turn right. When a car park and sea wall are seen on the right, descend to the wall and follow to the end. Turn left, up the ramp, turn right into High Street and continue to the town square.

HAMSTEAD FM

A

(S)

B

no-name FINGERBOARD

WEST HAMSTEAD FARM

WEST CLOSE

D

BOULDNOR COPSE

N

WOODED BAY

VICTORIA RD

E

YARMOUTH RD

CAR PARK

HIGH ST

F

Fingerboards
(A)(E) Coastal Path
(B)(C)(D) C.P. SI Yarmouth

## Hamstead Point and Newtown Estuary

The circular and sometimes muddy navigation of the Newtown River Estuary is rewarded by views of the coast, cliffs and estuary that are well worth the effort.
Hamstead ledge is a limestone outcrop of rocks that can be seen at low tide.

### Bouldnor Cliff and Copse

The copse is a thickly wooded Forestry Commission plantation which is home for, amongst others, the red squirrel.
If you stand quietly you may be rewarded with a glimpse of these rare creatures.

The seats on the cliff top clearings provide excellent view points.

The wooded bay is the last view point of the copse and tumbling cliff.

### Yarmouth.

As the name suggests the small town of Yarmouth stands at the mouth of the River Yar, or perhaps that should be the Western Yar, since the name also applies to another river on the Eastern side of the island at Bembridge.
The thriving harbour, of small boats makes for a colourful scene and for many the first stop on the island having sailed across the Solent on the Lymington Ferry.

The pier, built in 1876, was subsequently given a grade 2 listing in 1975 and renovated between 1984 to 86.
Marvellous views are gained by walking to the end of the pier.

# The Yarmouth File

**Yarmouth Castle** (from the pier) is one of the 16th century forts that Henry VIII had built to defend the Solent.

Yarmouth Pier

PIER TOLL 20p

NO BICYCLES BEYOND THIS POINT

# Section 3

## Yarmouth to Freshwater Bay

### 9 Miles

Y – Yarmouth
C.B – Colwell Bay
A.B. – Alum Bay
F.WB – Freshwater Bay

This is one of shortest sections of the walk, the reason being that the many features of this part of the Island, in our opinion, requires a slower pace so allowing many stops to photograph, look and listen.

From Yarmouth the route over Yar Bridge gives local views of Yarmouth Harbour and to the South and West a panorama of downland, some to be walked later.

Fort Victoria and the Country Park is a delightful woodland walk with a varied military history.

The Brambles Holiday Camp is an inland deviation before returning to the coast at Colwell Bay and 1½ miles of sea wall walking past, piers, rock outcrops, Coastguard Stations and a variety of sitting, looking and drinking points.

The steep, steps up Widdick Chine and gradual climb on to Headon Hill are rewarded with 360° views.

Alum Bay is a buzz with activity, and includes many interesting features such as monuments, the coloured sands and an assortment of displays.

From Alum Bay, the path continues toward the Needles and up on to the West High Down.

The history and views, the Needles seem so near, from the Needles Old Battery make a worthy deviation before the down. After the gentle climb from the Needles to Tennyson Down the highest point has been reached and with it one of the best views of the Island, Mainland and Solent.

A similar gentle descent awaits for Freshwater Bay and the conclusion of this section.

(23)

# Yarmouth to Cliff Road

Leave Yarmouth by the Yar Bridge and follow the road until a left hand bend, (Fb-A) turn right to the sea-wall. Turn left, along the wall until a wooded path on the left is taken to Westhill Lane. Turn right and then left (Fb-B) onto the woodland path behind Fort Victoria. Stay on this path, past the view point, and through a fenced section to Monks Lane. Turn left and follow the road to the entrance of Brambles Chine Holiday Camp. Turn right (Fb-c) down the main access road and then left alongside the white walled, and then hedge lined path to the 3 way fingerboard, (Fb-d) at the top of Brambles Chine.

Two routes are now possible :-

R1... continue along the track to the road. Turn right and follow to Colwell Chine Rd, turn right to the sea wall.

R2...
**Tide and weather permitting**
Turn right, through the chine, to the beach. Turn left and re-join the sea wall. Routes re-joined .... Follow the sea wall past Warden Point, Totland Pier, and the beach cafes to the old Lifeboat Station where a steep path, just after, is taken up the cliff to emerge on Cliff Road.

### Fingerboards
(A) P.F.P. Ft (6) Victoria Pk / seawall)
(B) C.F.P F6 Colwell Bay 1½ via Victoria Park
(C) C.R.P. F9 Colwell, Totland, Alum Bay
(D) **3 way board.**
  P.F.P. F13 Beach and Colwell (tide permitting)
  C.R.P F10 Totland / Yarmouth Rd ¼ mile

FORT VICTORIA

STEPS

WESTHILL LANE

STEPS

FENCED SECTION

MONKS LANE

HOLIDAY CAMP

LINSTONE CHINE

BRAMBLES CHINE

COLWELL CHING RD

WARDEN POINT

TOTLAND PIER

GATE

OLD LIFEBOAT STN. STEPS

YAR BRIDGE

N

# Fort Victoria Country Park.

Defending the Solent and hence the harbours of Southampton and Portsmouth has always been a priority.

Two main building periods are evident, that of Henry the VIII in the 1540s, and the Victorians in the 1850s.

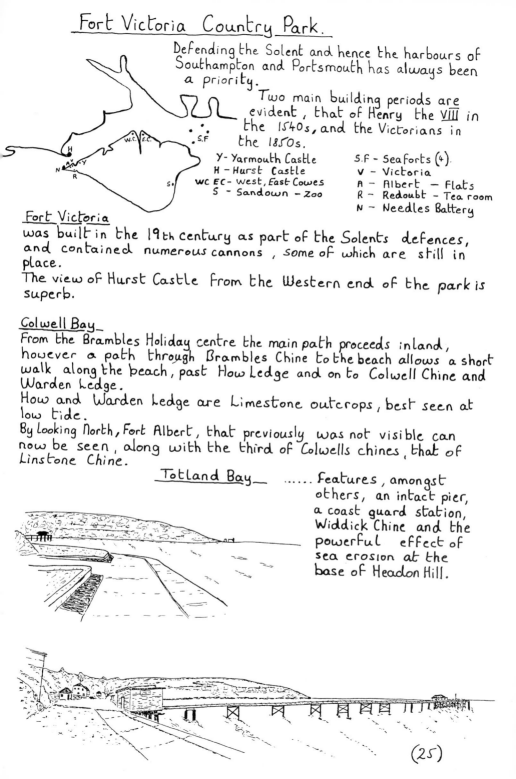

Y - Yarmouth Castle
H - Hurst Castle
WC EC - West, East Cowes
S - Sandown - Zoo

S.F - Seaforts (4).
V - Victoria
A - Albert — Flats
R - Redoubt - Tea room
N - Needles Battery

## Fort Victoria

was built in the 19th century as part of the Solents defences, and contained numerous cannons, some of which are still in place.

The view of Hurst Castle from the Western end of the park is superb.

## Colwell Bay

From the Brambles Holiday centre the main path proceeds inland, however a path through Brambles Chine to the beach allows a short walk along the beach, past How Ledge and on to Colwell Chine and Warden Ledge.

How and Warden Ledge are Limestone outcrops, best seen at low tide.

By looking North, Fort Albert, that previously was not visible can now be seen, along with the third of Colwells chines, that of Linstone Chine.

### Totland Bay

...... features, amongst others, an intact pier, a coast guard station, Widdick Chine and the powerful effect of sea erosion at the base of Headon Hill.

(25)

# Cliff Road to Tennyson Down

Turn right and follow the road until a fingerboard (Fb-A), on the right, returns you to the wooded cliff top path. On emerging from the woods bear to the left, and then right to climb Headon Hill where an assortment of paths cross the hill in an East-West direction. Leave Headon Hill by the zig zag path at the Western end, turn left at the gate, along the rough road, and then right along the main road to Alum Bay. On entering the Theme Park turn left and follow the road, through the park, and then around to the right (Fb-B) toward the Needles.

Approximately half way along the road take the steps and path to the left climbing the Down toward the Coastguard Cottages. On reaching the top of the Down turn left and, keeping to the centre path continue over West High Down. At the Footpath junction, beside the enclosed monuments take the half right path (Fb-c) for Tennyson Down.

↑ N

OLD LIFEBOAT STN

STEPS

CLIFF ROAD

⑤

A

POSTS

HEADON HILL

ENCLOSED MONUMENTS

TENNYSON DOWN.

Ⓕ

BURIAL MOUND

ZIG ZAG PATH

WEST HIGH DOWN

C

CAR PARK

B

BENT TREES

ALUM CHINE

MONUMENTS

COLOURED SANDS

COASTGUARD COTTAGES

THE NEEDLES

fingerboards
(A) P.F.P. to Alum Bay.
(B) C.F.P. T24a West High Down
(C) C.F.P. T25 Freshwater Bay & Tennyson Down.

# Headon Hill and Warren

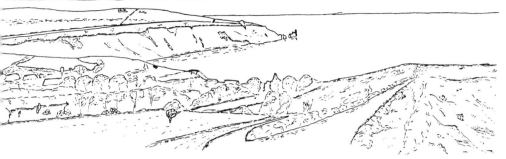

**Headon Hill** provides magnificent 360° views of the area and a variety of geographical features.

The effects of landslip from Hatherwood Point to Widdick Chine, contrast sharply with the coloured sand of Alum Bay and the white chalk cliffs toward the Needles peninsula.

A bronze age burial mound, dating to 1500 B.C. can be found on the top of Headon Hill.

### Signal Beacon
Situated on the cliff top, overlooking the bay is the wooden signal beacon, erected in 1988, to commemorate the sighting of the Spanish Armada in 1588.

## Marconi Monument
The square monument to the Italian Gugielmo Marconi can be found between the fun fair and car park of the Needles Theme Park. The monument marks the point of the Needles Wireless Telegraph Station from where " Marconi and British collaborators.....
.. experimented with wireless communications of all kinds."
The first messages were to a boat in Alum Bay, followed by Bournemouth 14 miles away, Poole 18 miles and finally ships 40 miles out to sea.

### Alum Bay
As a result of its coloured sands and views Alum Bay has become a very popular tourist spot.
The close up of the sands and white cliff makes the climb (steps) or chair lift to the beach worth while.

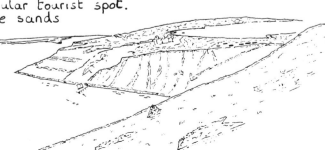

# Tennyson Down to Freshwater Bay

Continue over Tennyson Down.
On reaching Watcombe Bay turn left along the track,
and then right at the main road for Freshwater Bay.

The caves, at the foot of the cliff in Watcombe Bay

The "Little Needles" on the Eastern side of Freshwater Bay. Mermaid, Arch and Stag

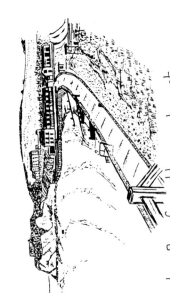

Freshwater Bay, from the wooden steps

N

TENNYSON MONUMENT

WATCOMBE BAY

FORT REDOUBT (TEA ROOMS)

FRESHWATER BAY

## West High Down

The gently
undulating
chalk down
is a haven
for wildlife
and vegetation,
which will show to the diligent observer.
It is interesting to note that the prevailing, and almost always
blowing, South West wind has caused numerous small trees to
bend, whilst the smaller and more malleable
bushes remain un-affected.

## Nodes Beacon

The Beacon was erected in 1785 on the top of
what is now Tennyson Down to act as
a warning to ships approaching the
Needles coastline of the dangers.
The function of the Beacon was
replaced in 1859 when the Needles
Lighthouse was built, so the site was
used for the Tennyson Monument.
The remains of the old Beacon and a
half size replica can be found in a
fenced enclosure to the West of the
Tennyson Monument.

## Tennyson Monument.

The monument was erected in 1897 to the poet Alfred
Tennyson and is on the highest point on the Down (482 ft).
As mentioned, it uses the site of the Old Nodes Beacon.

Beside the monument is a plinth which marks the point
of a beacon light, lit on 19th July 1988
to commemorate the sighting of the
Spanish Armada in 1588, some
400 years ago.
This is the second of the beacons
on this section of the walk, but
unlike the Alum Bay memorial, the
beacon has been replaced by a
flat top map board.

(29)

## Flat top Map Board.

D. DAY
LE HARVE 110   BEACH 102   CHERBOURG 71
DIEPPE 123                        St PETERS POINT 97

                                    USHART 241
BEACHY HEAD 78
                                    PORTLAND BILL 41
LONDON 88

SOUTHAMPTON 17                    HENGIST BURY HEAD 8
              HURST CASTLE 3

On a clear day the views (360°) are spectacular, with some 20 to 30 mile radius being easily within the scope of the naked eye.
From Southampton in the East to Swanage in the West, the Island, Solent and Southern mainland spread out like an enormous map.
If it is misty or for any other reason poor visibility then the above will be a fib!

### Watcombe Bay
The view from the clifftop path shows two caves being cut from the chalk cliff, by the sea. This process is happening all along the headland,

### Fort Redoubt
was built by the Victorians in the 19th Century due to the possible threat of French invasion.
It is now a tea room, with excellent views.

### Freshwater. Bay
Positioned neatly between Tennyson Down and Afton Down, the bay is an excellent conclusion to the days travels.

### St Agnes Church
built in 1908 has a thatched roof, and can be found along Gate Lane.

(30)

# Section 4
# Freshwater Bay to Chale

F.W.B

**11 Miles**

C - Compton
S - Shippards
B - Brook
C - Chilton (Iow Pearl)
G.M - Grange & Marsh
B.H - Barnes High
BA - Barnes chine

Co - Cowleaze
SH - Shepherds
WH - Whale
L - Ladder
W - Walpen

After yesterdays relatively short walk and exploration of the Western part of the Island, the route now takes a far more remote and dramatic course over the South West Cliffs to Chale.

Do be careful, and heed any notices, changes of path and common sense etc, because the rate of cliff erosion can quickly make a path unsafe and directions inaccurate. For this reason we have not included fingerboards in this section to avoid possible confusion, however they are present.

From Freshwater Bay the path climbs steeply over Compton Down, past the three chalk stacks and then down to Compton Bay, where the path follows the cliff top wherever possible with the occasional inland detour to navigate a chine.
From Compton Chine the views of coast and Shippards Chine, Hanover Point with fossilized logs on the beach, and Brook Chine are an excellent start to a day of cliff walking.
Chiltern Chine has the Isle of Wight Pearl beside it.
Grange and Marsh Chine is a Y shaped chasm, crossed at the bottom on a little bridge.
Barnes Chine is easily missed, Barnes High is not and gives a wonderful sitting and looking seat.
Cowleaze and Shepherds Chines sandwich the Holiday Camp between them.
Whale Chine is spectacular, but dont miss Ladder and Walpen Chines before todays conclusion at the pretty village of Chale.

(31)

# Freshwater Bay to Brook Chine

From the bay proceed along the sea wall, up the steps and on to the cliff path. Continue past the three chalk stacks and slowly climb Afton Down until the road and path run side by side on a chalk and grass embankment. As the road turns inland turn right over a stile, and steps, and cross the field with the plank bridge in the middle, over Compton Chine.

Cross the next stile and follow the path between fence and cliff top to Shippards Chine.

Cross Shippards Chine by the path and steps, go through the car park to the stiles and cliff top path. Continue along the path, past Hanover Point, to Brook Chine. Turn left to the road, through a car park, turn right along the road, and right again over a cattle grid and back toward the coast with the cottages on your left.

The wreck of the Tug Priscilla in Compton Bay.

The coast toward Brook Chine, from Hanover Point. On the beach are the remains of fossilized tree trunks.

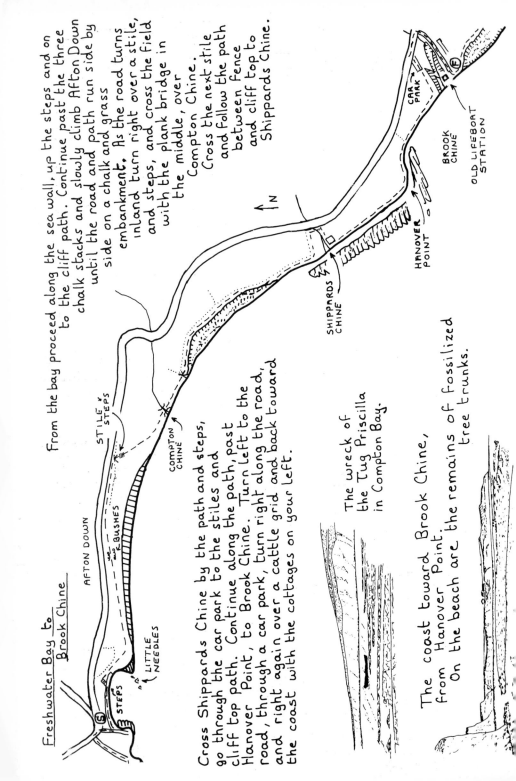

AFTON DOWN

STILE & STEPS

COMPTON CHINE

BUSHES

LITTLE NEEDLES

STEPS

S

N

SHIPPARDS CHINE

HANOVER POINT

CAR PARK

BROOK CHINE

OLD LIFEBOAT STATION

F

## Freshwater Bay

The bay features sea erosion in all of its phases, from the formation of caves on the Western cliff, to arches and stacks on the East and finally the clearing of the whole cliff being the bay itself.

The three chalk stacks on the Eastern side of the bay are sometimes referred to as the Little Needles and have been named individually as Mermaid, Arch and Stag.

Looking at the layering and bedding planes of the three stacks poses an interesting thought about Stag, in that the horizontal layering of Mermaid and Arch are not consistent with the 45° layering of Stag. Could it be that Stag is a piece of fallen cliff top? If in the minds eye the rock is moved through 45° and positioned on to the cliff face the layering appears to re-align ..... just a thought.

## Shippards Chine

Demonstrates the characteristic V shape and dramatic erosion

## Compton Bay

## Brook Chine.

The chine gives easy access to the coast, and was the launching point for the Brook Lifeboat in the 19th century.

# Brook Chine to Grange and Marsh Chine.

Turn left along the cliff top path to Chilton Chine. Turn left, through the bushes and car park, to the road. Turn right, past the Isle of Wight Pearl, and then right beside the hedge, to return to the cliff top path.
Turn left, past the holiday camp and continue to Grange and Marsh Chine. Cross the chine by the track, path, and footbridge followed by a scramble up the other side to the stile and continuing coastal path.

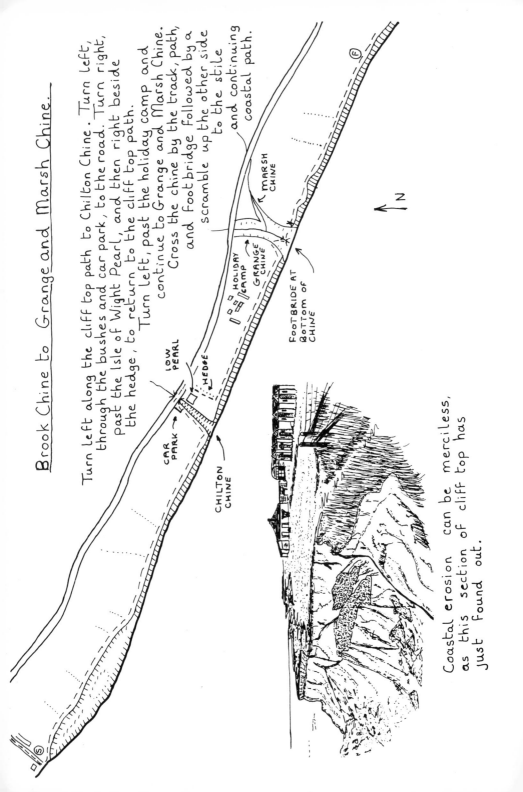

CAR PARK

LOW PEARL

HEDGE

CHILTON CHINE

HOLIDAY CAMP

GRANGE CHINE

FOOTBRIDGE AT BOTTOM OF CHINE

MARSH CHINE

N

Coastal erosion can be merciless, as this section of cliff top has just found out.

## Chilton Chine

is a characteristically steep sided chine with no access to the beach, and is bordered by the Isle of Wight Pearl.

At low water it is possible to see Hardman Rock, being part of the outcrop that runs between Compton Bay and Brightstone Bay.

This stretch of coast that faces South West receives the full force of the prevailing winds and sea onto its hazardous coast of underwater rock outcrops, some extending out to sea and many miles down the coast.

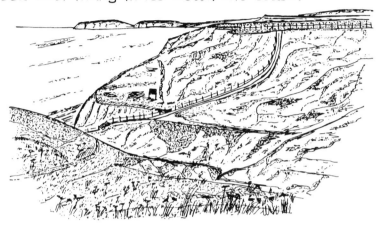

## Grange and Marsh Chines

This chine, or chines, is wider than the previous, the reason being that two streams have formed two chines that have then joined to form the present Y shape.

It was here, that in May 1799 the vessel "Les Deux Amis" was beached by a combination of bad weather and poor repairs carried out before the voyage.

Many vessels have become victims of the combination of the weather, rough sea's, rocks and poor visibility. Even after the ship is beached or grounded, getting off the beach by the abandoning crew is still a problem as the cliffs are near sheer, leaving only the chines for escape.

(35)

## Grange and Marsh Chine to Ladder Chine

Continue to Barnes Chine, then climb Barnes High (trig point on your left) and on to Cowleaze Chine. Turn left to the head of the chine and then right to cross in front of the holiday camp and on to Shepherds Chine.

Cross the chine by descending the path, follow the bank of the stream to a convenient crossing point and then climbing up the other side.

Continue along the cliff path, past the Coastguard Station on the left and Atherfield Point on the right to Whale Chine. Turn left to the road, turn right along the road, and right again beyond the car park for the cliff path, and Ladder Chine. Turn left for Walpen Chine.

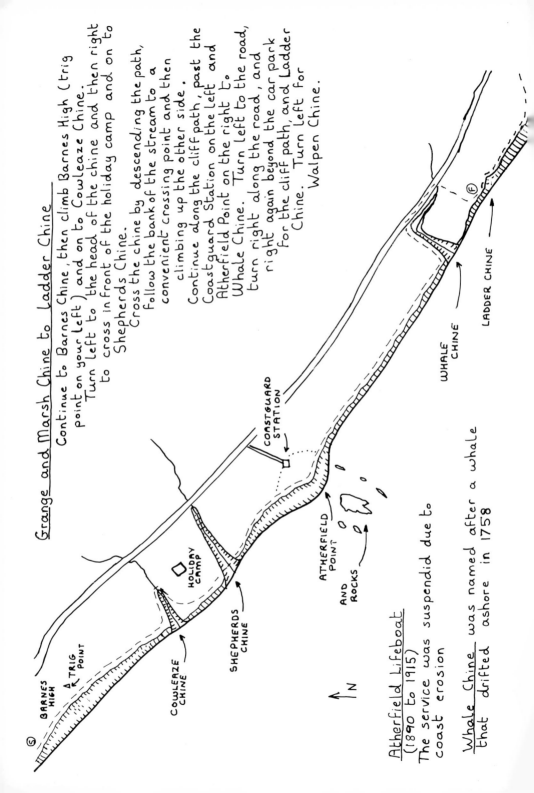

BARNES HIGH

TRIG POINT

COWLEAZE CHINE

HOLIDAY CAMP

SHEPHERDS CHINE

COASTGUARD STATION

ATHERFIELD POINT AND ROCKS

WHALE CHINE

LADDER CHINE

N

## Atherfield Lifeboat
(1890 to 1915)

The service was suspendid due to coast erosion

Whale Chine was named after a whale that drifted ashore in 1758

## Atherfield Ledge

Between Shepherds and Whale chine is Atherfield Point, from which, at low tide the Limestone outcrop of Atherfield Ledge can be seen.

As with most outcrops there is a great deal more of the rock under the water than above, and as such the currents and tides are affected.

Like others, Atherfield Ledge has been responsible for many shipwrecks, one of which was the Alcester which in February of 1897 ran on to the rocks, and

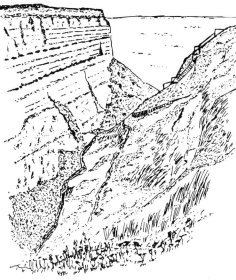

subsequently broke in two as tugs tried to pull her free.

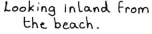

## Whale Chine
(four views of, or from!)

Whale Chine is a deeply eroded chine that has a good deal of vegetation in its sheltered inland area. The erosion near the cliff edge is dramatic to the point that on one trip, features noted were over the edge by the next

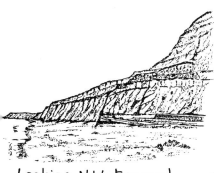

Looking inland from the beach.

Looking N.W toward Atherfield Point

(37)

Looking S.E. toward St Catherines Point.

# Walpen Chine to Chale

From the chine cross the plank bridge and turn left, (Fb-A) along the edge of the field until the corner. Turn left over the plank bridge and stile and then right to emerge via a hedge lined field onto a road. Turn right for the village of Chale.

## Fingerboards

(A) Coastal Path

CHALE

THE TERRACE

WALPEN CHINE

BLACKGANG CHINE

N

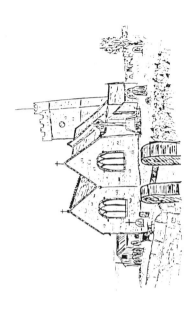

ST Andrews Church    Chale

# Ladder and Walpen Chines.

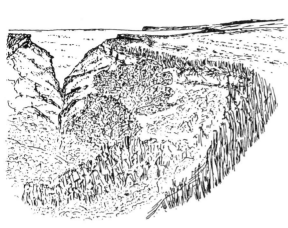

The last, for today anyway, of the now familiar V shaped chines.
Equally dramatic is the first good view of Blackgang Chine, Gore Cliff and Niton Down.

## Village of Chale

What a wonderful location for a village, the Downs behind and coastal views for 15 miles, or more, in front.
The village is mentioned in the Doomsday Book and has a focal point of the Church of Saint Andrews, dating from the 12th Century.

The graveyard of the church contains a stone, which is just readable, to the victims of the Clarendon.

In October 1836 the Clarendon was on the last leg of a voyage from the West Indies when navigation problems and bad weather drove the ship ashore at Blackgang.

## Natural Features

At the end of a section containing so many geographical and geological features perhaps an explanation of a couple is in order.

### The formation of Stacks, in a Headland

Fig 1 The sea attacks the base of the chalk cliff and will find the weakest point

Fig 2 The sea works its way into the cliff to form caves.

Fig 3 The continued action of the sea forces the cave openings outward and upwards until a weak roof is left to the cave.

Fig 4 When the roof of the cave falls in an arch is formed.

Fig 5 When the roof of the arch falls in stacks are left. These in turn will be eroded.

Evidence of cave formation (fig 2) can be seen in Watcombe Bay and the cliff below Fort Redoubt in Freshwater Bay.
Evidence of arch and stack (fig 4 & 5) formation can be seen on the Eastern side of Freshwater Bay.

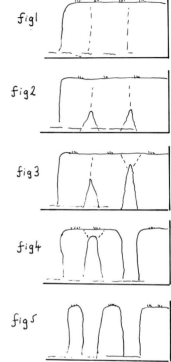

fig 1

fig 2

fig 3

fig 4

fig 5

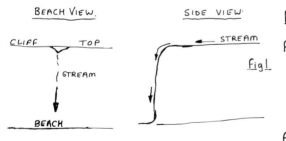

BEACH VIEW.

CLIFF    TOP

STREAM

BEACH

SIDE VIEW

STREAM

fig 1

CLIFF    TOP

V gorge formed by stream

fig 2

NEW COURSE OF STREAM

### Formation of a Chine

Fig 1 When a stream flows over a soft rock cliff to the beach below back cutting of the rock begins.

Fig 2 As the erosion and back cutting continues the characteristic V shape will form, as will the length and depth of the chine

(40)

# Section 5
# Chale to Sandown

## 12 Miles

C - Chale
N - Niton
SL - ST Lawrence
V - Ventnor
L - Luccombe
SH - Shanklin
SA - Sandown

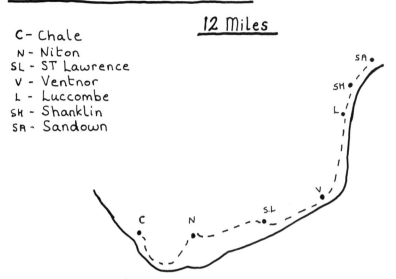

From the charming village of Chale the path climbs on to
the inland cliff and follows it past Niton and on to
St Lawrence where a swop is made for the Undercliff
path.
The high path gives good views of the Undercliff, including
ST Catherines point and lighthouse, whilst the Undercliff
path compliments with views of the massive inland
cliffs.
From Woody Bay to Ventnor is a lesson in coastal erosion
with and without man's help.
From the pier, and amusing fingerboard, the new sea
wall gives easy walking to Bonchurch and its secluded
church.
At the time of writing a continuation of the sea wall means
that the little path to the church may be missed, so look
out for the fingerboard by the pottery.
The Landslip, with its fallen trees and "home made" paths
has to be followed with a reasonable sense of direction,
although the path, boarded in places, basically follows
the cliff line, gradually climbing to the track for
Luccombe.
   A Wishing Seat (rock), two tea rooms, one chine, and
plenty of woods and seaviews later is the road to
Shanklin.
Decision time! — the upper or lower route to Sandown.(41)

# Chale Church to St Lawrence Masts

From the church, cross the road into The Terrace and then left (Fb-A) along the fenced path to the road. Turn right, along the road, and around to the left. As the road bends to the right gate posts will be seen on your right. Go through and turn immediately left following the line of the field, to a corner where a path will be found that climbs to a car park. Turn right, through the car park, up some steps (Fb-B) and on to Gore Cliff. Turn left and follow the path to the masts above St Catherines Point. Continue on the now hedge lined path through two fields and down a rough track called Boxers Lane to the main road at Niton.

Turn right, along the road, and then left (Fb-C) up a track. At the junction turn right (Fb-D) and then left (Fb-E) along a hedge lined path to emerge overlooking the Undercliff on your right. Stay on the cliff top path (Fb-F) as it weaves its way between hedge, field and cliff edge until the masts are reached. Cross the stile and field to the Fourway Fingerboard.

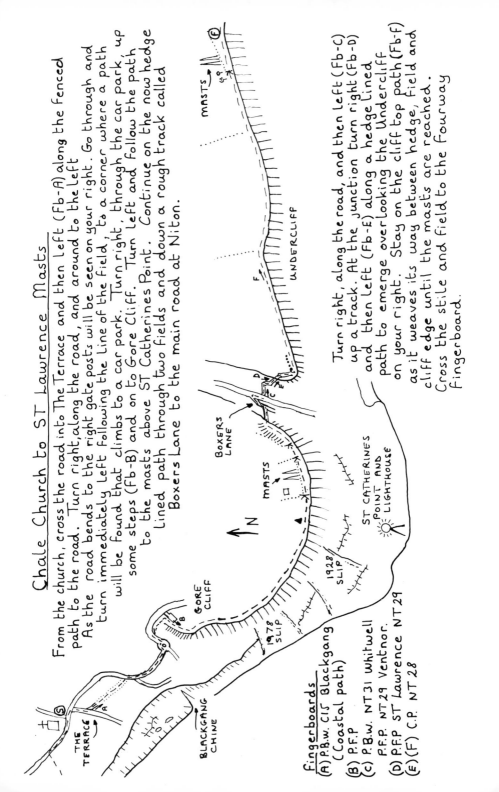

THE TERRACE

BLACKGANG CHINE

GORE CLIFF

1978 SLIP

1928 SLIP

MASTS

ST CATHERINES POINT AND LIGHTHOUSE

BOXERS LANE

N

MASTS

UNDERCLIFF

## Fingerboards
(A) P.B.w. CIS Blackgang (Coastal path)
(B) P.F.P
(C) P.B.w. NT 31 Whitwell
    P.F.P. NT 29 Ventnor.
(D) P.F.P St Lawrence NT 29
(E) (F) C.P. NT 28

## Blackgang Chine

The Chine has been predominantly taken over by the Theme Park, however spectacular views are possible from the end of The Terrace in Chale, and the cliff top to the East of Blackgang.

Blackgang Chine gets its name from the gang of smugglers who used the easy access to the sea to transport contraband goods.

The use of many of the chines, for smuggling, was very common in the 18th Century and the resultant confrontations between Excise Men, as they were known then, and smugglers were often violent, since both penalty and profit were high.

On St Catherines Down, reached by the path from the car park, are the original **attempts** at Lighthouses for this coast.

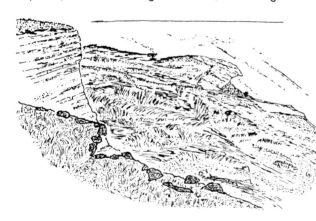

### Gore Cliff and Windy Corner

From this point the views of the South-West Coast speak for themselves.

A picture board map, in the car park, shows the names of the chines, hills, villages and coastline within view.

### The Glanville Fritillary

is a unique butterfly found only along the Southern coast of the Island.

### ST Catherines Point and Lighthouse

Beneath the waves of ST Catherines Point, lies numerous rock ridges that rise perilously close to the surface, without actually breaking, and a gully running parallel with the land of great depth. The necessity for a lighthouse has been evident for many years, and the present lighthouse, built in 1836 continues the task.

(43)

# ST Lawrence Masts to Ventnor Sea Wall

Turn right at the fourway fingerboard (Fb-A), down the steps to ST Lawrence. Turn left, along Seven Sisters Road, and then right into Spindlers Road which is followed to the road junction. Cross over to Old Park Road and follow around. Turn left into Woolverton Road. Look for a gate (Fb-B) and path to the right for Woody Bay. Cross two stiles to a track, turn left across the field to a gate. Turn right (Fb-c) along the track to the steps at Woody point. Follow the coast path as it weaves past Sir Richards Cove, and the animal pens (Fb-D) to the steps at Steephill Cove. Climb the steps and turn right along the path passing the cricket green on your left. When you reach the road, turn right and follow around to the left, past garages on the left, this leads into a footpath which emerges into a car park above Ventnor Esplanade. Follow the road down to the esplanade and along to the pier. Stay on the seawall (Fb-E), past the Water Gardens, and follow to the end at Bonchurch.

Fingerboards
(A) C.P. V81 ST Lawrence (Steps)
(B) P.F.P.
(C) C.P. Diversion
(D) P.F.P. V80 Steephill Cove, Ventnor.
(E) New Seawalk, Bonchurch

# Woody Bay

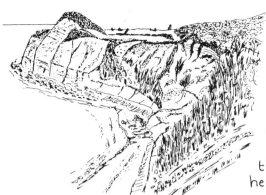

The path has been re-routed around the bay, the original passing across the, now battered shoreline.

From the steps the views are of ST Catherines Point, and lighthouse to the S.W, the bays and Ventnor to the N.E and the inland cliff to the N. The bays, Woody, Sir Richards and Steephill, all demonstrate the sea's power to erode, and hence the path weaves.

## Ventnor

Like ST Lawrence, Ventnor is built on the Undercliff, with the High Cliff flanking to the North, and the ever approaching sea to the South.

Ventnors coastline has been shored-up by the promenade and more recent building of the seawall to Bonchurch (April 88)
The coast between Steephill Cove and Ventnor is protected by large blocks of limestone installed at the base of the cliff, an example of which is passed before the cliff top car park.
(A 6 Tonne block of Limestone from the Mendip Hills that is full of fossils.)

On the sea front is a clock and meteorological station and on the occasions that we were there, the Midday Gun was fired from the Spy Glass Inn P.H.

A water garden, opposite the now sadly damaged pier, displays a plaque to Edgar Harvey the designer of the gardens. It is these spa waters that allowed Ventnor to grow in popularity, during Victorian times.

Ventnor is also the last place to lose its rail link, the line originally ran to Shanklin and further stations.

Ventnor was also tried as a harbour but the vicious sea's and treacherous coast made it unsuccessful.

(45)

# Ventnor Sea Wall to Shanklin

The path (Fb-A) is on your left alongside some houses. Climb the steps and follow the wooded path to the church. Turn right (Fb-B) and follow the edge of the playing Field to the steps, then along the track past Carigdene Farm (Fb-C) and into the wooded Landslip area. Follow the path as it twists and turns through the woodland, slowly climbing, to emerge via some steps onto track.

Stay on the track to Dunnose Cottage, on the left, and the track to Luccombe Chine, on the right. Bear right and cross the track on to the foot path (Fb-D) and follow, past the tea garden to the junction with Luccombe Road. Turn left (Fb-E) and follow this road to Popham Road.

Two routes are now possible

R1 - Cross Popham Rd and follow the foot path, past the chine entrance and up to the old Village of Shanklin. Return to the cliff top by Chine Ave.

R2 - From the junction turn right to the top of Applysteps, which are then descended to the beach. Turn left along the beach to the road.

## Fingerboards.
(A) P.F.P. to Old Church & Village
(B) P.F.P. to Landslip & Shanklin
(C) F.P. Landslip
(D) C.P. SS2 Luccombe
(E) Coastal Path

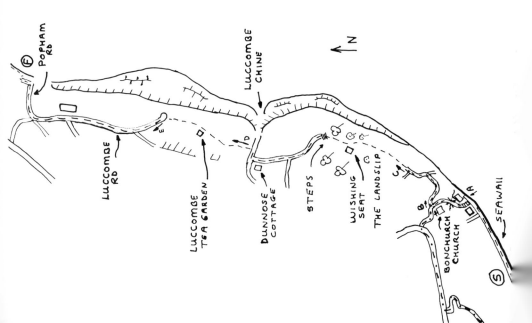

## Bonchurch Old Church

The wonderful setting of this little church is worthy of an elongated pause to sit and look. The church is of Norman build, although built on the ruins of an earlier Saxon Church.

## The Landslip

It is the natural sandwich like layering of the muds and sands, combined with a gentle inclination toward the coast that has produced the area known as the Landslip.

This layering from bottom to top, consists of, Sandrock Beds and Carstone, these being members of the Lower Greensand group, Gault Clay, Upper Greensand and in some cases a layer of Chalk to top.

The movement is caused by rain water percolating down through the relatively porous Chalk and Upper Greensands until the Gault Clay is met. The Clay slowly becomes saturated and lubricated with water until a rotation slipping in the

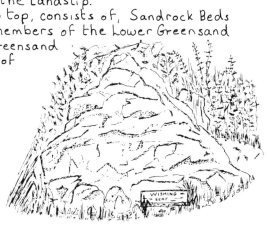

clay occurs and the cliff face rotates and falls seaward. Explanations apart, the Coastal Path route is a marvellous walk through this area.

### Luccombe

The path does not enter the village but two tea rooms, and a chine worthy of the detour. mark our route card.

Shanklin pier and Sandown Bay from Appley Steps.

(47)

## Shanklin to Sandown Pier

At the road junction, two routes are again possible.

R1 – Continue along the sea front to where the road finishes and then take the beach promenade to its conclusion at Sandown Pier.

R2 – From the roundabout turn sharp left up the hill to Chine Inn P.H. Turn right and follow the clifftop path along Eastcliffe Promenade, over Hope Road and along the path ultimately descending the steps on to the promenade beside Sandown Pier.

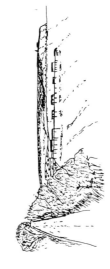

Sandown Pier from Eastcliffe Promenade.

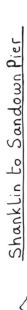

N

EASTCLIFFE PROMENADE

BEACH PROMENADE

HOPE RD

SHANKLIN PIER

SHANKLIN CHINE

APPLEY STEPS

SHANKLIN OLD VILLAGE

S

The Luccombe Road allows panoramic views of Shanklin, Lake, and Sandown along with the surrounding Downs and Sandown Bay.

Left.. Sandown Bay from Luccombe Rd.

## Shanklin

is a Victorian seaside town, with its pier built in the late 19th Century, that is now damaged.
The old village is worthy of a detour for its quaintness, as is the chine which can be reached from the old village or the shore.

Shanklin was one of the exit points of "PLUTO" which stands for Pipe Line Under The Ocean and was used to supply fuel to the Allies after the D.Day landings of World War Two.

It was at the top of Appley Steps that we overheard a gentleman telling a small boy that this is where .......

Above ... knock Cliff and Horse Ledge

......" the pipeline FIDO went to France". Thank you sir.

Above... the beach promenade, Shanklin to Sandown

Left.... Sandown Pier

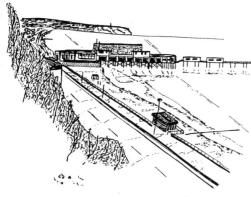

(49)

# Shanklin Old Town

Thatched cottages, pubs and tourist shops line Church Rd, which runs through the centre of the Old Village.

Just off the main road is the head of Shanklin Chine, with its waterfall and secluded garden walk.

Since leaving Ryde and covering some 58 miles this is the first time that a rail link has been available. Not so, a few years ago when the Island had a comprehensive rail network spreading in all directions.

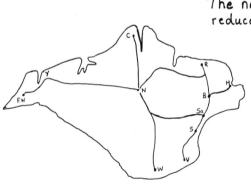

The network has dramatically reduced, now making access to the Western and Southern Island somewhat more difficult, although a proportion of the tracks have been removed and the routes turned in to paths. eg Freshwater Way (in parts)

C - Cowes
N - Newport
F.W - Freshwater
R - Ryde
B - Brading
H - St Helens

Sa - Sandown
S - Shanklin
V - Ventnor
W - Whitwell
Y - Yarmouth

# Section 6
# Sandown to Ryde

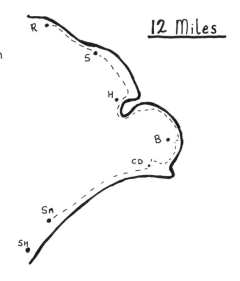

**12 Miles**

SA - Sandown
CD - Culver Down
B - Bembridge
H - ST Helens
S - Seaview
R - Ryde

After Sandown its back to the coast with Red Cliff and Culver Down to start the day.

The views from Culver Down are spectacular and although not as high as Tennyson Down do offer the other side of the "ariel map" first seen on the Western peninsular.

Whitecliff Bay is shelted and the woodland path a delight as the clifftop path proceeds to Bembridge.

Bembridge has variety, the cliff top and views of the rock ledges, the life boat house, and a harbour with a history of its own.

ST Helens Causeway is a unique experience.... dont miss it.

.....so is the Old ST Helens Church, just off the Coast Path.

From Seaview to Ryde the sea wall and path are followed with unobscured views of the Solent and Mainland.

At low tide the large expanse of Ryde East Sands are constantly in the foreground, and as the tide comes in, are rapidly covered as the sea comes up to the wall, indeed caution should be exercised between Puckpool and Ryde.

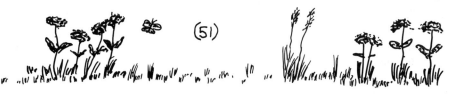

# Sandown Pier to Whitecliff Bay

From the pier, follow the seafront to the end and turn left into Avenue Slipway. Turn right at the junction and turn left into Avenue Slipway. Turn right at the junction and continue along the sea wall, past the amusements and Iow Zoo, on your left, until a car park on the right. Go through the car park and join the path on the coastal side of the sailing club. Stay on the clifftop as you climb Red Cliff. and the two fields, before reaching Culver Down. Cross the road beside the Coastguard kiosk, through the gate, and turn half right (Fb-A) across the field, past the Earl of Yarborough monument. On reaching a broken fence turn right. At the next junction of paths and fences turn left, down a path and then some steps. Follow the clifftop path as it weaves around Whitecliff Bay.

## fingerboards
(A) P.F.P. BB29 Brading.

WHITECLIFF BAY

(F)

YARBOROUGH MONUMENT

COASTGUARD KIOSK

POSTS

RED CLIFF

HOLIDAY CAMP

SAILING CLUB

CAR PARK

IOW ZOO

BOAT POND

AVENUE SLIPWAY

GEOLOGY MUSEUM

N

S

Red Cliff and Culver Down.

## Sandown

Like so many towns as we see them now, their original purpose has altered, Sandown being no exception.
The towns origins, come from the defence building days of the mid 19th century, the Isle of Wight Zoo being a converted fort.
The town is a popular sea-side resort, and has been for many years, due to its sheltered beach and facilities.
A walk to the end of the pier provides excellent views of both towns that cannot now, sadly be seen from Shanklin pier.

## The Isle of Wight Geology Museum

is in Sandown and provides a fascinating insight to the pre-history of the island.

## The Red Cliff

is a small outcrop of Lower Greensand and Wealdon Clay which, as can be seen on the beach, is easily eroded.
The cliff provides a stark colour contrast with the white of Culver Down, in the same way that Compton Bay did with Afton Down on the S.W. Coast.

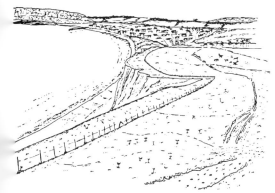

## Culver Down

Is part of the chalk ridge that runs across the Island from East to West, and along with many views and much wild life is home to a memorial to Charles Pelham, the Earl of Yarborough.
A commemoration signal beacon, to the sighting of the Armada in 1588 can be found at the Eastern end of the down, along with splendid views.

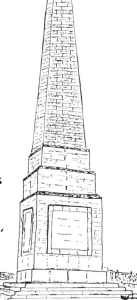

(53)

# Whitecliff Bay to St Helens Causeway—

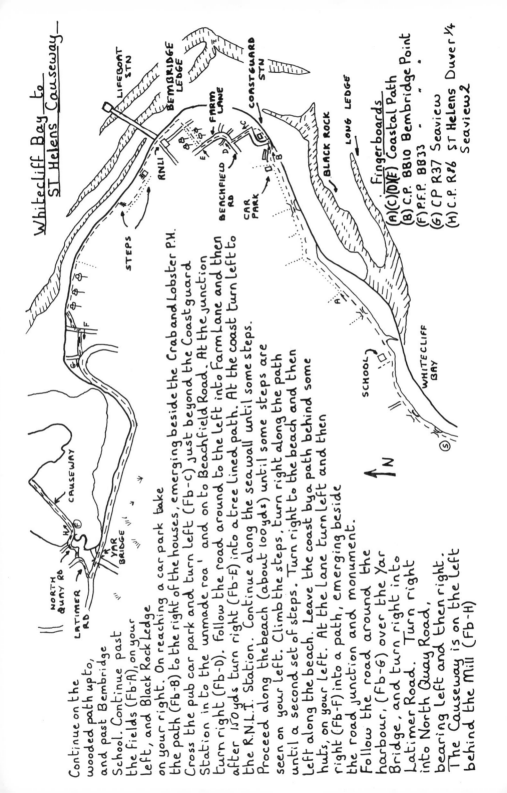

Continue on the wooded path up to, and past Bembridge School. Continue past the fields (Fb-A), on your left, and Black Rock Ledge on your right. On reaching a car park take the path (Fb-B) to the right of the houses, emerging beside the Crab and Lobster P.H. Cross the pub car park and turn left (Fb-c) just beyond the Coastguard Station into the unmade road ' and on to Beachfield Road. At the junction turn right (Fb-D). Follow the road around to the left into Farm Lane and then after 150yds turn right (Fb-E) into a tree lined path. At the coast turn left to the R.N.L.I. Station. Continue along the seawall until some steps.

Proceed along the beach (about 100yds) until some steps are seen on your left. Climb the steps, turn right along the path until a second set of steps. Turn right to the beach and then left along the beach. Leave the coast by a path behind some huts, on your left. At the lane turn left and then right (Fb-F) into a path, emerging beside the road junction and monument.

Follow the road around the harbour, (Fb-G) over the Yar Bridge, and turn right into Latimer Road. Turn right into North Quay Road, bearing left and then right. The Causeway is on the left behind the Mill (Fb-H)

↑ N

## Fingerboards

(A)(C)(D)(E) Coastal Path
(B) C.P. BB10 Bembridge Point
(F) P.F.P. BB33
(G) CP R37 Seaview
(H) C.P. R86 St Helens Duver ¼
                    Seaview 2

WHITECLIFF BAY

SCHOOL

LONG LEDGE

BLACK ROCK

CAR PARK

BEACHFIELD RD

FARM LANE

COASTGUARD STN

RNLI

BEMBRIDGE LEDGE

LIFEBOAT STN

STEPS

CAUSEWAY

NORTH QUAY RD

LATIMER RD

YAR BRIDGE

## Whitecliff Bay

Easy walking and easy views, with a remarkable similarity to its opposite number on the Western coast.

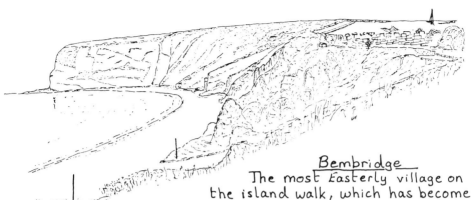

## Bembridge

The most Easterly village on the island walk, which has become a hive of activity, principally because of the Victorians, both with its residential estates and holiday activities.

At low tide the limestone rock outcrops of Long Ledge, Black Rock and Bembridge Ledge can be seen.

These rocks, along with further off shore obstacles, are a real danger to boats and the presence of the Coastguard and R.N.L.I Stations would seem to support the frequency with which assistance is required.

## Bembridge R.N.L.I.

By having the long pier to the boat shed, a launch can be achieved regardless of high or low tide.

(55)

# ST Helens Causeway to Toll Road

On leaving the Causeway continue in the same direction, over the grass and along a road. At the left hand bend take the path opposite (Fb-A) and keep to the right hand side of the field. At the next stile turn right, through some bushes, and then half left to climb and exit the field by the gate, onto a road. Turn right (Fb-b) and continue. Just beyond the gates of the Priory Hotel turn left (Fb-c) along the treelined path which is followed to the end. Turn right along the path, track, lane to the coast. Turn left along a path, (Fb-D) beside the toilets, and continue as it turns from path into a track and then road. (Pier Road). Turn right down High Street to the sea wall, follow around to the left. As the road bears inland the sea wall is on the right and is followed to Toll Road.

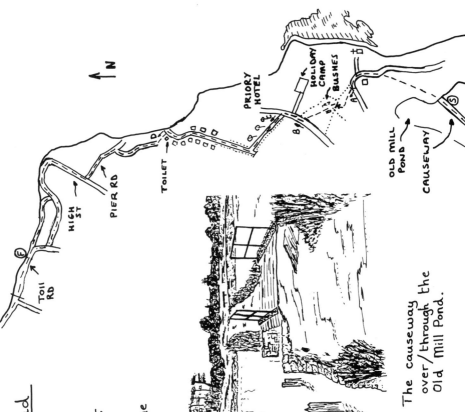

The causeway over/through the Old Mill Pond.

## Fingerboards

(A) c.p. P.F.P. R85 Nettlestone, Seaview 1½
(B) c.p. R84 Seaview
(c) c.p. P.B.w. R84 Seaview
(D) c.F.P. R101 Seaview½ Ryde 2½

## Bembridge Harbour

The Harbour, as we see it now, is a relatively recent sight since the water once extended to Brading. This inland estuary was formed by the flood water of the last ice-age and the now land locked village at Brading was once a port.

Since the first attempts to bridge the estuary, many-land reclamation and draining projects have been undertaken with a variety of success and failure until the present situation, built in 1878.

The B3395 bridges the harbour leaving Brading high and dry, and Bembridge and ST Helens as harbour villages.

The harbour although tidal, has a supply of fresh water from the River Yar.

## The Old Mill Pond

It is a strange feeling, to say the least, to walk across a harbour on dry land.

The purpose of the pond was to fill and hold the water, ready for use at the water mill.

By using this proced-ure a constant supply of water was available on a fill up and drain basis.

## ST Helens

By deviating to the coast, the remains of the 12th century Church of ST Helens can be found along with coastal views of Nodes Point to the North and Bembridge Point to the South, that are not possible once the main path is re-joined.

## Seaview

As the name suggests the views are extensive of Mainland, Solent and forts.

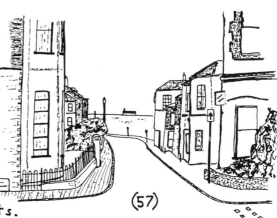

# Toll Road to Ryde Pier

Continue along Toll Road as it leads into Springvale Road.
At the left hand bend the sea wall is taken past
Puckpool Point and Appley Tower to Ryde promenade.
Continue along the promenade, past the boating
Lake on your left, and the new centre, on your right,
to the pier.

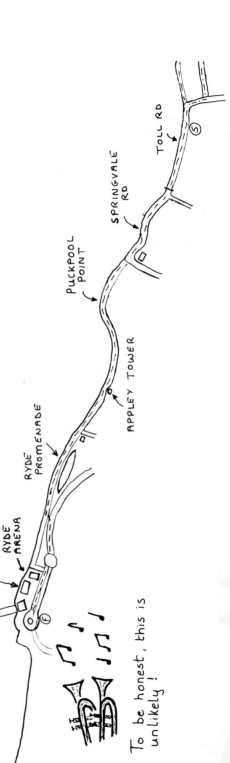

TOLL RD

SPRINGVALE
RD

PUCKPOOL
POINT

APPLEY TOWER

RYDE
PROMENADE

RYDE
ARENA

Bus STN

To be honest, this is
unlikely!

## Seaview... cont.

The Forts that can be seen in the Solent, of which there are four were installed as a precaution against attack by the French.

These fears proved unfounded, however the then Prime Minister, Lord Palmerston took them seriously and had massive defences built all around the Island, a number of which are seen on the Coastal Path.

The forts were subsequently used in the Second World War by attaching submarine booms, and hence their original purpose of protecting the Solent Harbours was finally realised some 60 years after their construction.

Seaview also had a pier which was lost due to bad weather in 1951.

### Puckpool Point

Where the road and path separate there is a warning about high tides, so if necessary, a deviation through Appley Park should be made.
With the tide out the extent of Ryde East Sands can be seen.

The coast between Puckpool Point (above) and Seaview (left)

### Appley Tower

Built as a watch tower by Sir William Hutt, it is the last of the sitting, and looking spots before Ryde.

Behind the tower is a stone commemorating the first fleet of ships sailing to Australia in 1787 from this shoreline.

1½ miles to go!

# View point  Culver Down.

Looking North over the North East Island and Southern Mainland.

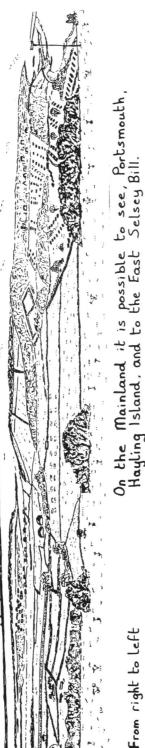

On the Mainland it is possible to see, Portsmouth,
Hayling Island, and to the East Selsey Bill.

The hills in the far distance
are the South Downs.

**From right to left**

Whitecliff Bay
Long Ledge
Black Rock
Bembridge Ledge
Bembridge Village
Bembridge Harbour
ST Helens
Seaview,
and just off the picture Ryde

**Right** — The coast at Bembridge,
Looking N.W. toward
Bembridge Point.

## Ryde

Having gone full circle an opportunity now exists for a further exploration of Ryde.

The notes on page 7 still apply, but a wander around the town will reveal much more.

Appley Tower and
Puckpool Point.

Ryde Pier, from the East Sands.

Well, thats it three years of research, walking and drawing comes to an end, and we loved every minute of it.
If you are reading this on the ferry back to Portsmouth from Ryde, having walked the whole route, then congratulations, whether you are a veteran of many long distance paths, or a first timer your achievement is to be applauded.
We hope that in the case of this 70 mile circumnavigation you have enjoyed the small slice of features and places mentioned.

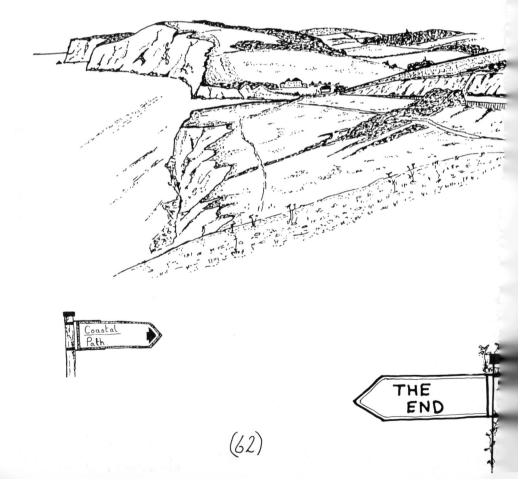

Coastal Path

THE END

# Notes